ABC
CHRISTMAS

ABC CHRISTMAS

Learn the alphabet with Christmas!

P.G. Hibbert

Angel

Bow

Candy Cane

Drum

Elf

Family

Gingerbread

Holly

Icicle

Jingle

Kris Kringle

Lights

Mittens

NORTH POLE
SANTA'S WORKSHOP
Reindeer Crossing
Elf Village
MRS. Claus's Kitchen
SLEIGH RIDES

North Pole

Ornaments

Presents

Quilt

Reindeer

Snowman

Tree

Ugly Christmas Sweater

Village

Wreath

X-Mas

Yew

Zebra with a Christmas Hat